Explore 24 Series

S0-CNE-536

Yumderful Cooking Activities

by Kim Carlson

Dear Chef,

Cooking can be a lot of fun, but before you begin, there are a few simple rules to remember:

1. Always ask an adult before using the kitchen.
2. Read the recipe twice to make sure you understand it all before beginning to cook.
3. Make sure you have all of the necessary ingredients before you start.
4. Wash your hands before you touch food and after you are done.
5. Always clean up when you are finished.
6. Make sure you aren't allergic to any of the ingredients in a recipe before you begin.
7. Never put food into the oven without an adult helping you.
8. Never take hot food out of the oven or microwave without an adult helping you.
9. Have fun!

Sincerely,
Kim Carlson

P.S. To help you get started, we have placed the appropriate icons (seen below) on each recipe. They can help you decide if the recipe is easy to make, quick, one that requires adult help, and so on.

Quick   Easy   No Electricity   Toaster   Adult Help   Microwave

Editorial: Kristy Kugler, Paul Rawlins
Art and Design: Andy Carlson, Robyn Funk, Magen Mitchell, Amanda Sorensen

© 2006, Rainbow Bridge Publishing, Greensboro, North Carolina 27425. The purchase of this material entitles the buyer to reproduce worksheets and activities for classroom use only—not for commercial resale. Reproduction of these materials for an entire school or district is prohibited. No part of this book may be reproduced (except as noted above), stored in a retrieval system, or transmitted in any form or by any means (mechanically, electronically, recording, etc.) without the prior written consent of Carson-Dellosa Publishing Co., Inc.

Printed in the USA • All rights reserved.

ISBN 1-59441-720-2

Breakfast Facts

Little Miss Muffet

Little Miss Muffet, sat on a tuffet,
Eating her curds and whey;
Along came a spider,
Who sat down beside her
And frightened Miss Muffet away.

What exactly are curds and whey, anyway? Well, have you ever eaten cottage cheese? The lumpy bits are curds, and the liquid stuff is whey. The curds are milk proteins that lump together, and whey comes from the proteins that don't lump together. Whey doesn't taste very good—it's pretty sour and runny. So most modern-day cottage cheese is mostly curds with just a teeny bit of whey left in.

Breakfast Far Away

The typical German breakfast is very different from an American one. A common German breakfast (Frühstück) might be fresh bread or rolls from the local bakery with butter and jam or cheese. Sometimes the meal might include a slice of melon, a soft-boiled egg, or cereals.

Did you know? A common Japanese breakfast consists of hot steamed rice, miso soup (a soup made with tofu, green onion, seaweed, and broth), and dishes like fish, salad, or pickles!

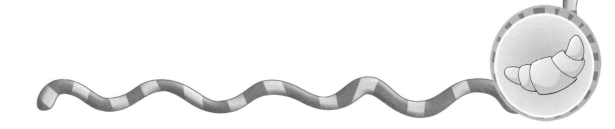

Breakfast Activities

Help Miss Muffet get to her tuffet so she can eat her curds and whey!

Lumpy Yogurt

1 cup of yogurt (you pick the flavor)
2 broken oatmeal cookies or 3/4 cup of granola

Don't you hate it when your cookies crumble? Well, don't throw them out! Mix the crumbs (or use your favorite granola mix) and your favorite yogurt together for a quick breakfast. Cookie crumbs taste great over frozen yogurt as well!

Variation: If you have some leftover fruit in the fridge—strawberries, blueberries, or raspberries, for example—toss bite-size pieces of the fruit in with your yogurt instead of using cookie crumbles or granola!

Quick

No Electricity

Easy

Activity
1

Pancake Rolls

1 pancake
1 sausage link or bacon strip

Take one homemade pancake, place a sausage link or bacon strip in the middle, and roll it up burrito-style. As a fun variation, you could add to or put on your pancakes: apples, berries, banana, nuts, coconut, or peanut butter. Now you have breakfast to go! Or, for an even better breakfast treat, put a little syrup in a dipping bowl and dip your pancake roll in the syrup. Yum!

Hop online and check out these fun pancake links:

THE OLNEY PANCAKE RACE:
http://www.sideburn.demon.co.uk/olney/pancake.html

INTERNATIONAL PANCAKE DAY:
http://www.swdtimes.com/pancakeday/content/history.html

FUN PANCAKE FACTS
http://www.funsocialstudies.learninghaven.com/articles/pancake.htm

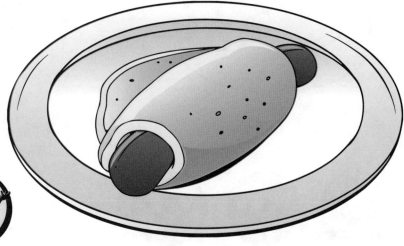

Quick   **No Electricity**   **Easy**

Wacky Waffles

2 toaster waffles
Your favorite jam or jelly
Your favorite fruit (like strawberries or bananas) sliced

Optional: peanut butter, maple syrup, or marshmallows—be creative!

Toast your waffles. Take all of your favorite ingredients listed above and spread them over 1 waffle. Cover the pile with the second waffle, and behold! Your wacky waffle awaits you! Eat with LOTS of emergency napkins nearby.

Quick

Toaster

Easy

Activity
2

Breakfast Burrito Buddies

1 scrambled egg
1 tortilla
1/2 cup grated cheese or 1 slice processed cheese
Your favorite breakfast foods (like potatoes, tomatoes, or avocados)

Food always tastes better when eaten with your fingers! Place a tortilla on a microwave-safe plate; then add all your favorite breakfast ingredients (mine are eggs, potatoes, black beans, and olives). Sprinkle with cheese. Fold the bottom of your tortilla over your food. Then tuck in one side and roll to the other. Leave the top open (it's easier to hold and roll that way). Microwave for 1 minute (maybe 2 minutes if your food came straight out of the fridge). Using hot pads, carefully remove the food from the microwave, or have an adult help you. Serve immediately. Don't forget the napkins!

Adult Help

Microwave

Easy

Hole-in-One

1 egg
1 slice of bread
butter

Cut out a hole in the middle of your bread with an upside-down glass. (Just press the glass into the center of the bread like a cookie-cutter and twist it a few times.) Butter the bread with the hole in it on both sides. Have an adult heat the frying pan for you. Carefully place the bread in the hot frying pan. Crack 1 egg into the hole (scramble it if you don't like a runny yolk). Cook for about 2 minutes or until you see the egg turning white on the edges. Flip the whole thing over and cook for another 1–1 1/2 minutes. Remove and enjoy!

Tip: Fry the middle circle of bread and dip it into the yolk to eat. Once you eat fried bread, you'll never want plain ol' toast again!

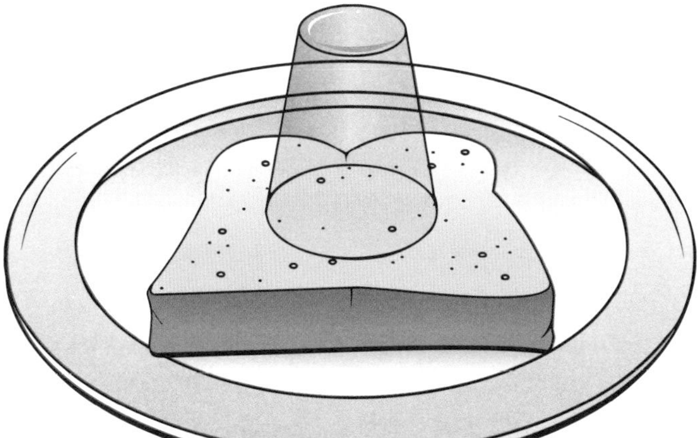

Adult Help

Easy

Activity

4

Lunch Facts

Hot Cross Buns

Hot Cross Buns! Hot Cross Buns!
One a penny,
Two a penny,
Hot Cross Buns!
If you have no daughters,
Pray give them to your sons!
One a penny,
Two a penny,
Hot Cross Buns!

Watch your manners!

Did you know that table rules change depending on where you are from? In America, it is common to ask for serving dishes to be passed to you so you can add food to your plate. In China, diners often eat directly from shared plates of food, using their chopsticks to handle the food. It is also okay to reach across the table to take a piece of food from a far-away dish. Saucers are often used to set bones and shells on or to rest a bite of food that was too big to be eaten at once.

In America, we eat most of our food with forks, spoons, and knives. In many parts of Asia, chopsticks and spoons are common eating utensils. In other places, it is perfectly acceptable to use your fingers, with things like bread to help catch juices and hold larger bites. Which method do you prefer?

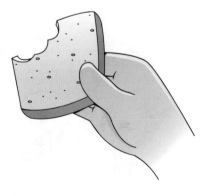

Lunch Activities

Draw and color the missing half of the hot cross bun.

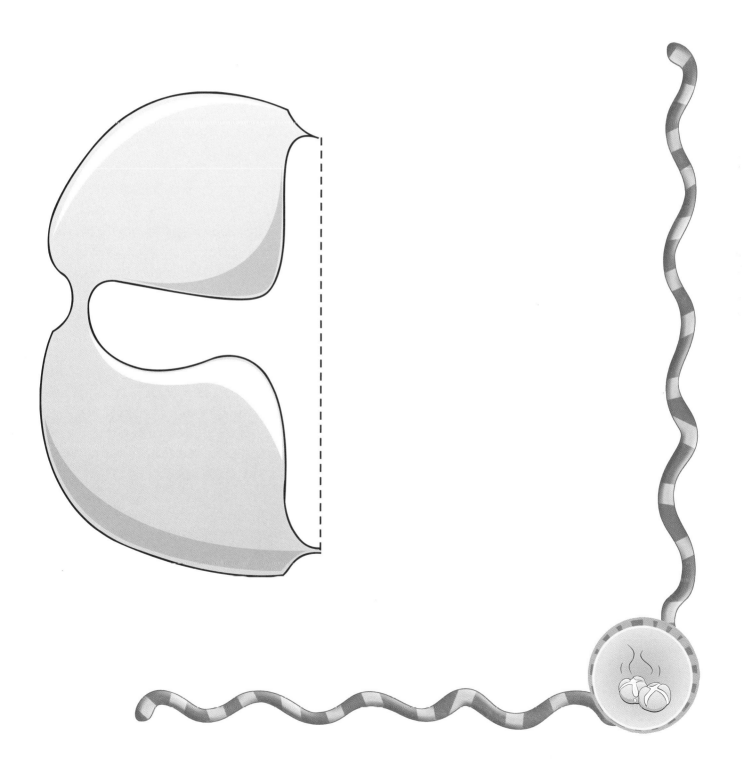

After-Easter Eggs

2 hardboiled eggs (especially colored ones)
1 tablespoon mayonnaise
1/4 teaspoon (or one good squirt) mustard
1/2 tablespoon relish (optional)
1 tomato
1/4 teaspoon oregano
dash of salt and pepper

Cut off the top of your tomato. Scoop out the innards (including the pulp and seeds) with a spoon and throw them away.

Take the shells off your eggs. Then mash the eggs in a bowl. Mix in the mayonnaise, mustard, and relish. Sprinkle with a little salt, pepper, and oregano. Spoon your egg mixture into your tomato and eat! Don't like tomato? Put the egg mixture on some avocado, or stuff a bell pepper instead. Add cucumber instead of relish if you like. Be creative!

No Electricity

Easy

Killer Quesadilla

2 tortillas
1 spoonful of refried beans
1/2 cup mozzarella cheese
1/4 cup salsa
1 spoonful sour cream

Place 1 tortilla on a microwave safe dish. Spread on the refried beans. Add cheese. (If you like spicy food, add a few sprinkles of hot sauce, too.) Cover with a second tortilla and microwave for 30–50 seconds. Cut tortilla into pizza wedges and pour salsa over the top. Plop on some sour cream in the middle, and it's ready to go! This is also good with the Cheater's Guacamole recipe on page 20! If you want a crispier quesadilla, have an adult help you cook it in the frying pan instead of the microwave, cooking the first side for 2 minutes and the second side for 1 minute.

Quick   **Microwave**   **Easy**

Activity
6

Pizzas Galore

Pick-a-Pita Pizza

1 whole pita
3–4 spoonfuls of spaghetti or tomato sauce
1/2 cup cheese
3 slices lunchmeat, diced

-OR-

1 whole pita
ketchup & mustard
1/2 cup cheese
3 sliced hot dogs

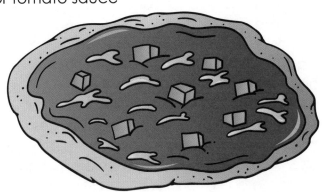

Place a pita on a microwave-safe plate. Add either the spaghetti sauce or the ketchup. Next, sprinkle on the lunchmeat or the hot dogs. Cover with cheese. Microwave for 1 minute or until cheese is melted. Cut into pizza slices and eat!

Pizza Babies

1 English muffin
2 spoonfuls of tomato sauce
Whatever you like on top of your pizza!

Toast the English muffin in the toaster. Spread the tomato sauce on each half of the muffin. Add whatever you like on your pizzas as toppings (suggestions: sliced mushrooms, oregano, and Swiss cheese). Microwave for 15 seconds, or have an adult put the muffin under a broiler for about 2 minutes. Wait until it cools a little before eating. Be creative: try zucchini or even scrambled eggs on top! You never know what your favorite combo will be until you try it!

Quick

Easy

Toaster

Microwave

T-N-T Sandwiches

2 slices of bread
1 can tuna (with all the water or oil squeezed out)
2 tablespoons mayonnaise
1 tablespoon relish (optional)
1/2 tomato, diced

In a bowl, mix the drained tuna, mayonnaise, and relish together. Slice a tomato in half and remove all the seeds with a spoon (so your sandwich won't be runny). Have an adult help you dice the tomato into small pieces and add it to the tuna mixture. Spoon some of the mixture onto 1 slice of bread and cover it with the second slice. Eat right away! Tuna mixture will stay fresh for 1 day if it is kept covered in the fridge.

Quick

Easy

Adult Help

No Electricity

Activity
8

A New Breed of Hot Dog

8 hot dogs
8 cooking skewers (soaked)
1 can crescent roll dough

Preheat oven to 375 degrees. Soak the skewers in water for about 10 minutes. This helps prevent slivers, makes the food slide on easier, and helps prevent burning. Skewer your hot dogs lengthwise. Take one triangle of crescent dough and wrap it around the hot dog until the hot dog is completely covered (overlapping is okay). Place your covered hot dogs on a cookie sheet (carefully—you don't want them to touch each other, or they'll stick together as they cook!). Have an adult put them in the oven. Bake the hot dogs for 10–13 minutes or until golden brown. Let them cool for about 5 minutes before eating.

Easy   **Adult Help**

Crispy Chicken Chunks

1 pound boneless, skinless
chicken pieces
1 egg
1 tablespoon olive oil
1/2 cup bread crumbs
2 cups rice cereal
2 teaspoons oregano
1 teaspoon garlic salt

Preheat oven to 325 degrees. Pour the rice cereal into a large resealable bag. Close the bag and make sure you squeeze all the air out. With a rolling pin or large wooden spoon, smash the cereal into smaller crumbs. Turn the bag over often while smashing. Once done, open the bag and add the bread crumbs, oregano, and garlic salt. Reseal the bag (don't squeeze the air out this time) and shake the mixture together. In a separate bowl, crack open the egg and add the olive oil. Mix well.

Prepare a large baking dish by covering the inside with foil and spraying non-stick spray all over it. Put several pieces of chicken in the egg-oil mixture. Coat the chicken pieces; then drop them in the bread crumb mixture. Close the bag and shake it up until the chicken is coated. Put the coated chicken in the baking dish in a single layer. Repeat until all the chicken is coated and in the pan.

Cover with foil and bake for 1 hour. Uncover and bake for another 20 minutes; then serve and eat.

Adult Help

Activity

9

Snack Facts

An Apple A Day

An apple a day keeps the doctor away.
Apple in the morning, Doctor's warning.
Roast apple at night starves the doctor outright.
Eat an apple going to bed, knock the doctor on the head.
Three each day, seven days a week—ruddy apple, ruddy cheek.

This rhyme was meant to encourage children to eat healthy foods—is it working?

Pizza

Pizza is an old dish, though tomatoes weren't added until after the discovery of America (tomatoes are native to the Americas). The first pizza didn't make it to America until the late 1800s, and pizza didn't really become a national favorite until the 1950s. The first frozen pizza didn't appear in grocery stores until 1957! Now pizza is the most popular frozen food around.

Snack Activities

Let's get the party started! Find your way through the maze to the snack food.

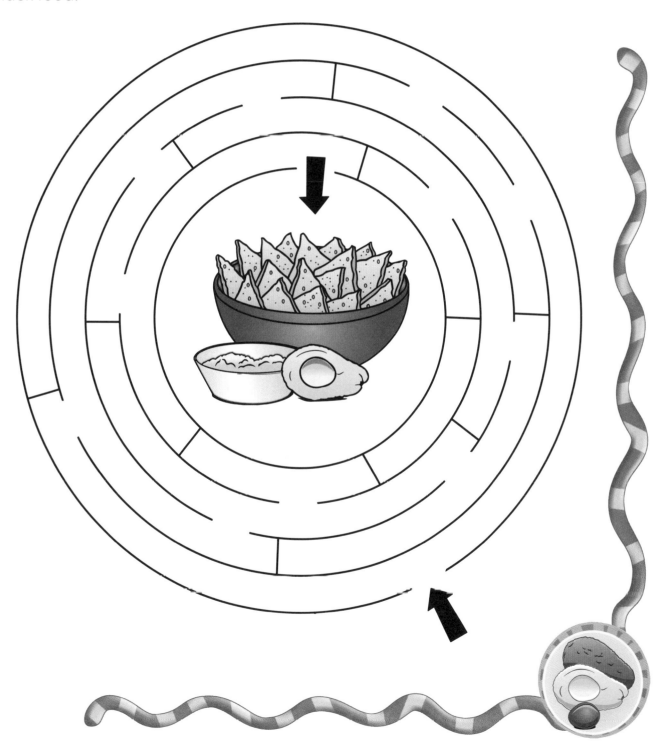

The Cheater's Guacamole

2 ripe avocados
1/4 cup salsa
1/4 teaspoon lemon juice

Peel 2 avocados and remove their pits. Smash them in a mixing bowl with a fork or a potato masher. Add salsa and lemon juice and mix together. Serve with chips or pour over your Killer Quesadilla (recipe on page 13)!

Quick

Easy

No Electricity

Mexican Porcupine

a handful of tortilla chips
1/2 avocado (peeled and seeded)
1/4 cup black beans
2 slices of processed cheese
1/8 cup sliced olives

Place your peeled half avocado flat-side down in the middle of your microwave-safe bowl. Stick your chips into the avocado. Pour your beans in between your chips. Sprinkle olives on top. Put 2 olives in front for eyes. Gently place your cheese slices on the very top of your porcupine. Microwave for 30 seconds to 1 minute or until cheese is melted. You can add salsa, sour cream, or even hummus to your porcupine, if you like!

Easy

Microwave

Activity
10

Small 'Sicles

1 can frozen juice concentrate
2 cups water
3–4 ice cube trays (depending on the size of your trays)
4 dozen toothpicks, or skewers cut to 2"

Mix your favorite frozen juice with the water just until lumps are gone. Pour it into the ice cube trays and place in the freezer. Make sure that the trays can sit flat so you avoid spills. After 3 hours, take them carefully out of the freezer. Place your sticks in the middle of each ice cube and return the trays to the freezer until the cubes are frozen solid.

OR

After you pour in the juice, place a strip of scotch tape over the top of each row of ice cubes (right in the middle). Make sure you don't get any juice on the tape. Once the tape is taut, poke the toothpicks through the tape and into the middle of each ice cube. Then place into freezer until the cubes are frozen solid. Take out your small 'sicles one at a time to enjoy.

Note: If the cubes are stuck, try running warm water on the bottom of the tray for a minute to loosen them.

Easy

Vampire Repellent

1 thick slice of French bread
2–3 teaspoons butter or margarine
1/8 teaspoon garlic salt
1/8 teaspoon Italian seasoning (optional)

Place your slice of bread in the toaster. When it's done, carefully take it out and butter one (or both) side(s). Sprinkle the garlic salt and seasonings over the toast. Make this dish whenever you need to avoid those pesky vampire guests.

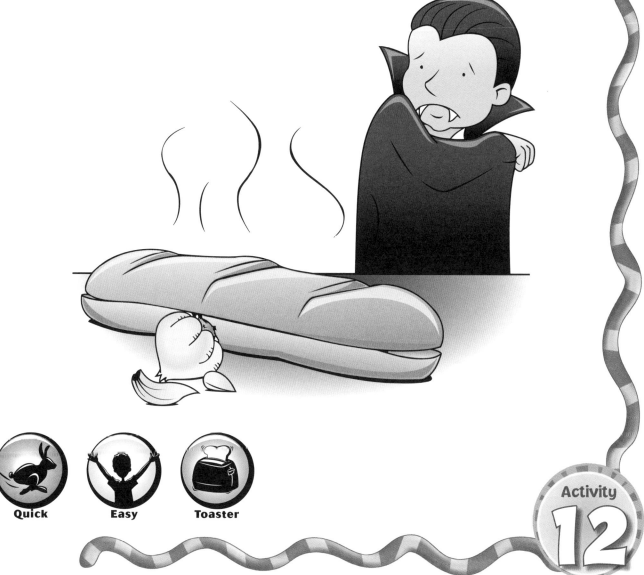

Quick   **Easy**   **Toaster**

Activity
12

Activity 13

Fruit Kebabs with Dip

12 wooden skewers (presoaked in water)
1 pound bite-size pieces of pineapple, apples, bananas, strawberries,
    watermelon, grapes, etc.
Fruit Dip (see below)

Soak skewers in water for about 10 minutes while you and an adult
cut up the fruit into bite-size pieces. Slide the fruit onto the skewers
until there's just enough room to hold the bottom of your stick.
Alternate types of fruit until you reach the top of the skewer. Serve
with a bowl of Fruit Dip (below). Dip skewers in the fruit dip and eat
one piece of fruit off at a time.

Fruit Dip

8 ounces of cream cheese (softened)
10 ounces (one can) of fat-free sweetened condensed milk
8 ounces (one tub) of whipped topping
2 teaspoons vanilla

Cream together the cream cheese and milk.
Add vanilla and whip until all lumps are
gone. Slowly fold in the whipped topping
and stir just until mixed. Don't
stir it too much!
Refrigerate for
1 hour before
serving. Stays good
for 1 week in the
fridge if properly
covered.

Adult Help

Easy

No Electricity

Fruit Sushi

4 square strips of fruit leather or fruit roll-ups
2/3 cup marshmallow crème
2 cups of your favorite sliced fruit (such as strawberries, apples, bananas)

Unroll the fruit leather or fruit roll-up square on a plate. Spread marshmallow crème all over the square. Start laying fruit slices in a row about 1 inch from the bottom of the square. Have the row of sliced fruit go all the way from the left to the right side of the square. Now it's time to roll your sushi! Hold the bottom 2 corners of the square and slowly lift and fold it over your fruit slices, rolling it all the way to the top. Cover with waxed paper and refrigerate for 1 hour.

When you are ready to eat them, take the fruit sushi rolls out of the fridge and place them on a plate. Have an adult carefully cut the sushi rolls into bite-size pieces for you.

Adult Help

Easy

No Electricity

Activity
13

Dinner Facts

Pease porridge hot!
Pease porridge cold!
Pease porridge in the pot
Nine days old.

Some like it hot,
Some like it cold,
Some like it in the pot
Nine days old!

Pease porridge is a food that is still eaten in Britain today. It's a smooth, thick, dark yellow sauce made from dried peas, and it is commonly served with boiled bacon.

Dinner Far Away

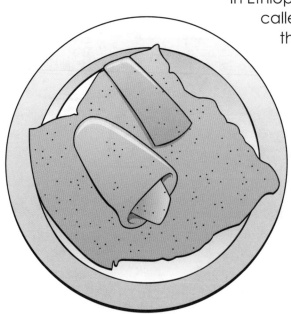

In Ethiopia, people eat a type of flat bread called <u>injera</u>. It's not just eaten with other things, however. Injera is also used as an eating utensil to scoop up meat and vegetable stews. It also serves as a sort of edible tablecloth, holding the food. Once the injera underneath the stew is eaten, the meal is over.

In Crete, the largest island of Greece, dinner is eaten no earlier than 9:00 p.m.! During the summer, midnight is often a very busy time at the restaurants.

Dinner Activities

Search Words

strawberry salad
cheesy pigs
cheesy worms

confetti meatloaf
oodles of noodles
veggies

no-bake casserole
pease porridge
evening

```
        d c l m
          u d m
          p i f
          x t
      r e y   a v   x i y r i
      l d y k o c e m k h i f j u c
    m w q g d o o s b x o w c o n h i
    p h c s b a d y b x w h v k s o h r
    y a u x g l l z a h q a a c f b m c m
  u c r c b w a e i v c x p s h o a e i m
  k b m t y h s s z x o x i n e w k v i w p
  n n i i b s y o b d n c r u e b e e t r n
  e u w h e e r f y p f m c g s f c n d x r
  i l i k y i r n j e e t h c y l a i p m c
  l v i f n g e o k a t b e h w i s n z l n
  w c z d i g b o w s t l e j o f s g t s f
  k m m j e w d m e i r s v r v e x n n
    z k o b v a l o p m l y e m g r h i r
    z k q v r e j o e q p z s n o k t
      x j a t s d r a u i e s m l e o
      i g z s u x r t l g j g i e s
      n i a w t i l y s t r b n
        j s s p d o d s w y c
        e v d g a y n o c
        r e e f w c s
        a y o w o
          y k
```

Strawberry Salad

4 fresh strawberries, sliced
1 cup fresh baby spinach, cleaned
1 tablespoon sunflower seeds

1 teaspoon strawberry jam
1 teaspoon balsamic vinegar
2 teaspoons olive oil

In a large salad bowl, mix together the jam, vinegar, and oil with a whisk. Next, add your spinach and strawberries. Toss together until mixed in well. Sprinkle sunflower seeds on top and serve.

Quick

Easy

No Electricity

Cheesy Pigs in Trees

1 ham steak cubed or 5 thick deli ham slices diced
1 head broccoli
1/2 pound cheddar cheese or 1 jar of cheese-whiz

Cover the bottom of a microwave-safe dish evenly with the ham.
Break little broccoli "trees" out of the head of broccoli and stick them
stalk-down into the ham. Pour or sprinkle the cheese over the top.
Cover with plastic wrap. Microwave for 10 minutes. Have an adult
help you remove the plastic wrap—Be careful! the steam will be HOT.
Let it cool for at least 2 minutes before serving.

Adult Help

Microwave

Easy

Quick

Activity
15

Cheesy Worms

1 package of ramen noodles or 2 cups of your favorite pasta noodles (cooked)
1 tablespoon butter or margarine
1/4 cup Parmesan cheese

Have an adult help you boil ramen noodles for 3 minutes, or microwave them in a large bowl with 2 1/2 cups of water for 5 minutes. If you prefer, you can boil some of your favorite pasta noodles instead. Drain completely and pour into a bowl. Add butter and cheese. Stir until all mixed together.

Note: This is also good with a little salt and pepper or fresh parsley, too.

Adult Help

Easy

Quick

Confetti Meatloaf

1 shredded carrot
4 broccoli florets diced teeny-tiny
5 medium sized mushrooms diced teeny-tiny
1 small onion diced
1/2 cup bread crumbs
2 tablespoons ketchup
1 tablespoon Worcestershire sauce or soy sauce
1 pound ground hamburger or turkey

Preheat oven to 350 degrees. Wash your hands really, really well before you start and after you finish. Dump all of the ingredients listed above into a mixing bowl. Use your hands to smoosh it all together. Place in a greased loaf pan or any baking dish at least 2" deep. Cover with foil. Bake the meatloaf for 1 hour to 1 hour and 20 minutes. Have an adult help you take it out of the oven and serve.

Adult Help

Easy

Activity

17

Oodles of Noodles

1 package of large seashell noodles
1 8-ounce package of cream cheese
1 cup shredded mozzarella cheese
1 tablespoon Italian seasoning (or oregano and parsley)
1 teaspoon garlic salt
1 jar spaghetti sauce or Alfredo sauce

Boil noodles as directed on package. Drain in a colander and pour cold water over the noodles to cool them off and stop the cooking process. While the noodles are boiling, put the softened cream cheese in a large mixing bowl and smash it until it is good and mushy. Add cheese, seasonings, and garlic salt and mix together. Pour a couple of spoonfuls of sauce in the bottom of a 9 x 13 baking dish. When the noodles have cooled enough to handle them, hold a seashell noodle in one hand and scoop a spoonful of cheesy mixture with the other hand. Stuff your noodle and place it in the baking dish. Repeat until all noodles are stuffed. Pour the remainder of the sauce on top of the noodles. Add extra cheese on top if you wish. Cover with foil. Have an adult bake it in the oven for 30–35 minutes at 375° F.

For a complete meal, serve this with Vampire Repellent (recipe found on page 23)!

Adult Help

Volumes of Veggies

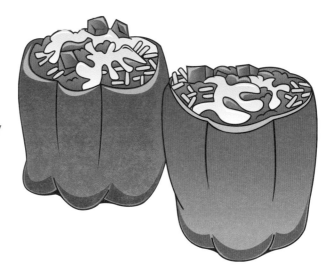

2 bell peppers
1 small onion, diced
1 shredded carrot
1 cup diced broccoli
1/2 pound ground hamburger or turkey
1 cup cooked rice
1 1/2 cups shredded cheese
1 tablespoon ketchup
1 teaspoon garlic powder
salt and pepper

Have an adult help you cook the
ground meat and onions in a frying pan. Once they are cooked
through, remove the pan from the heat and add all remaining
veggies and rice. Mix together with ketchup, garlic powder, salt,
pepper, and 1 cup of the cheese. Set aside to cool off. Cover a
cookie sheet with foil. Cut the tops off the bell peppers and remove
the seeds and veins (the white strips inside). Stuff the peppers with the
meat and veggie mixture and place on the cookie sheet. Sprinkle the
rest of your cheese on top. Have an adult help you bake the peppers
in a 400-degree oven for 5–10 minutes (until cheese is melted). If you
need to serve 4 people, cut the peppers in half from top to bottom
and fill each half with the mixture instead. You can also add chili
powder to spice up your meat.

Don't like broccoli? Try zucchini or tomatoes instead. Don't like bell
peppers? You can stuff tomatoes instead!

Adult Help

Activity
19

No-Bake Casserole

1 12-ounce package of egg noodles
1 can cream of mushroom or cream of celery soup
1 can peas
4 ounces cream cheese, cut into cubes
1 teaspoon Italian seasoning (or parsley and oregano)
dash of salt and pepper and garlic powder

Boil noodles as directed on package. Remove noodles from water and drain in a colander. While the noodles are draining, return the pan to the stove and turn the heat to low. Spray the inside of the pan with non-stick spray (I recommend butter flavor or olive oil). Add cream cheese cubes and creamed soup. Return hot noodles to the pan and stir until the cream cheese melts and isn't lumpy anymore. Add peas and seasonings, then cover and turn heat off. Let the mixture sit for about 5 minutes before serving.

Note: For a delicious variation, add 1 can of tuna (drained) or cooked chicken or ham.

Adult Help   **Easy**

Dessert Facts

Simple Simon met a pieman going to the fair;
Said Simple Simon to the pieman, "Let me taste your ware."
Said the pieman to Simple Simon, "Show me first your penny."
Said Simple Simon to the pieman, "Sir, I have not any!"

A long time ago, fairs were a great place for street vendors (sellers) to sell their food (or wares) to people. People didn't have fast food restaurants then. So Simple Simon was going to the fair when he met a man who was selling pies. Sadly, poor Simple Simon was a bit short on cash!

Dessert Far Away—Lassi

Lassi is India's version of the milk shake. It's a cold yogurt drink mixed with ice and various flavors. You can find sweet lassi (often made with mango) or salty lassi (made with things like cumin and cardamom).

Chocolate

Some of the most famous chocolate today is made in Europe. But Europeans had never heard of chocolate until they began exploring the Americas. The cacao tree is native to South America. Columbus brought cocoa beans back to Europe, but it wasn't until Montezuma gave the Spanish explorer Cortez the drink "chocolatl" that Europeans began to understand chocolate's potential. The Aztec drink was bitter, so Cortez and his men added cane sugar to sweeten it. This was the beginning of a chocolate revolution!

Dessert Activities

Use the alphabet code below to solve these tasty riddles!

Q. What's a cat's favorite dessert?

A. $\underline{}$ $\underline{}$ $\underline{}$ $\underline{}$ $\underline{}$ $\underline{}$ $\underline{}$ $\underline{}$ $\underline{}$ $\quad$ $\underline{}$ $\underline{}$ $\underline{}$ $\underline{}$ $\underline{}$!
    3   8   15   3   15   12   1   20   5   13   15   21   19   5

Q. What is a lemming's favorite dessert?

A. $\underline{}$ $\underline{}$ $\underline{}$ $\underline{}$ $\underline{}$ $\underline{}$ $\underline{}$ $\quad$ $\underline{}$ $\underline{}$ $\underline{}$ $\underline{}$ $\underline{}$ $\underline{}$ $\underline{}$
    12   5   13   13   9   14   7   13   5   18   9   14   7   21   5

$\underline{}$ $\underline{}$ $\underline{}$!
 16   9   5

Q. What do ghosts serve their guests for dessert?

A. $\underline{}$ $\quad$ $\underline{}$ $\underline{}$ $\underline{}$ $\underline{}$ $\underline{}$ $\underline{}$!
  9   19   3   18   5   1   13

Q. Why didn't the Thanksgiving turkey eat dessert?

A. $\underline{}$ $\underline{}$ $\quad$ $\underline{}$ $\underline{}$ $\underline{}$ $\quad$ $\underline{}$ $\underline{}$ $\underline{}$ $\underline{}$ $\underline{}$ $\underline{}$ $\underline{}$!
  8   5   23   1   19   19   20   21   6   6   5   4

Q. What's another name for a bug dessert?

A. $\underline{}$ $\quad$ $\underline{}$ $\underline{}$ $\underline{}$ $\quad$ $\underline{}$ $\underline{}$ $\underline{}$!
  1   6   12   25   16   9   5

A	B	C	D	E	F	G	H	I	J	K	L	M
1	2	3	4	5	6	7	8	9	10	11	12	13

N	O	P	Q	R	S	T	U	V	W	X	Y	Z
14	15	16	17	18	19	20	21	22	23	24	25	26

Gone Fishin'

1 package of blueberry gelatin
a handful of gummy or Swedish fish and sharks
2 cups of grapes
2–3 strips of fruit leather
1 very clean fishbowl

Arrange grapes in the bottom of your clean fishbowl. Mix the gelatin as directed on the package and pour it in the fishbowl. Gently slide in the fruit leather to look like seaweed. Drop in your gummy fish and sharks. Place in the fridge for 1–2 hours until set. If you find all your fish have sunk to the bottom (which sometimes happens), add a couple more after the first 30 minutes in the fridge. This is great for birthday parties!

Hint: Want to have smaller, individual fishbowls? Empty baby food jars work great! Enjoy fishin'!

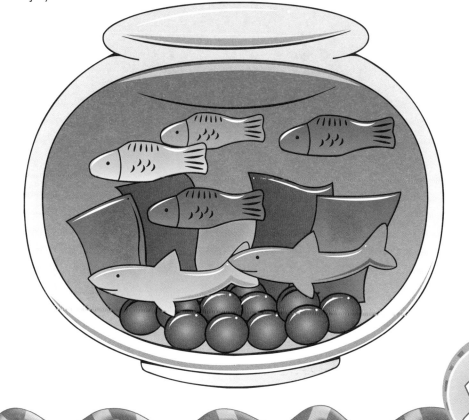

Easy

Activity
21

Some More S'mores

chocolate cupcake mix
12 large marshmallows

Follow the directions for your favorite cupcake mix/recipe. Grease cupcake trays or spray non-stick spray on the bottoms of paper cupcake cups. Fill each cup 2/3 full. Set 1 marshmallow right in the center of the batter. Have an adult help you bake the cupcakes as directed on the recipe. Remove the cupcakes from the tray immediately after you take them out of the oven and let the cupcakes cool for just a few minutes. Serve while they are still warm.

The marshmallow makes a nice crispy topping while staying ooey-gooey inside. If you prefer, you can cover the marshmallow completely with the batter and just ice the cupcakes instead. But remember, they are best eaten warm!

Adult Help

Easy

Quick

Chocolate Cure-All

1 bag chocolate chips
12 vanilla wafer cookies OR chocolate chip cookies OR
   12 strawberries OR 2 bananas (peeled) OR ... (be creative!)

Pour the chocolate chips into a deep, microwave-safe bowl and microwave for 15 seconds. Stir and microwave for another 10 seconds. If chocolate chips are still not melted, microwave for another 7 seconds. Stir again and dip your cookies or fruit (or both) into the chocolate and lay them on a piece of waxed paper to cool. Keep working until you are done. If the melted chocolate begins to cool off before you are finished, just microwave it in 7-second intervals until re-melted.

Hint: Butterscotch chips are yummy, too!

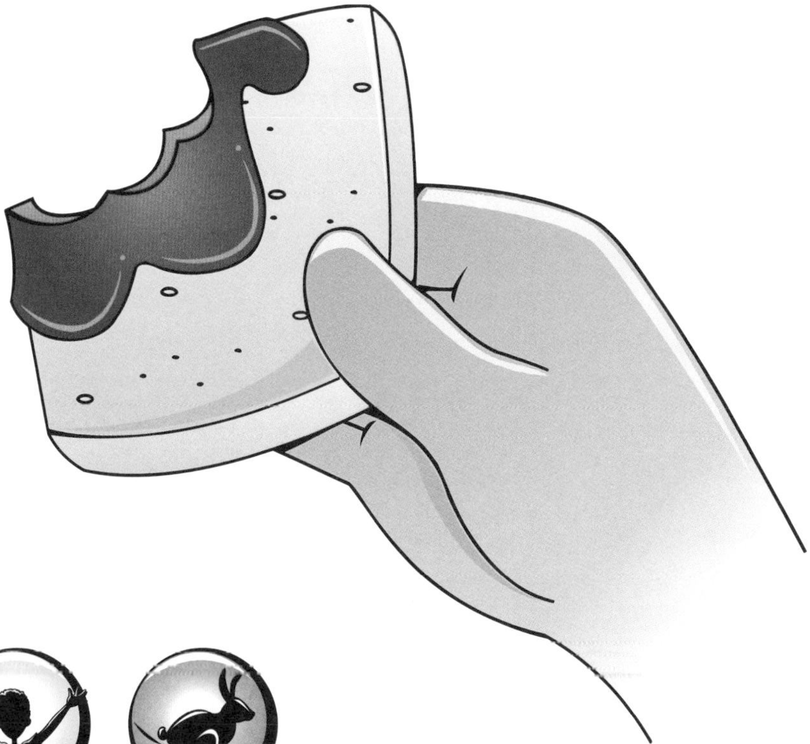

Adult Help   Easy   Quick

Activity
22

Apple Trails

4 apples (cored)
4 tablespoons peanut butter
2 cups granola mix
1 teaspoon sugar
1 teaspoon cinnamon
1/4 teaspoon nutmeg

Ask an adult to core your apples almost, but not quite, to the bottom. In a bowl, mix together all remaining ingredients (note: you may omit the peanut butter if you wish). Divide your mixture evenly into fourths and stuff each apple. Put them in a baggie, and you are ready to hit the hiking trails!

On a winter's day, this is a great treat to heat in a 350-degree oven for 25–30 minutes. Drizzle a little maple syrup on top and enjoy!

Adult Help

Easy

Quick

No Electricity

The Best Oatmeal Cookies on the Planet!

1 cup butter or margarine
1 cup brown sugar
1/2 cup sugar
3 egg whites
1 1/2 teaspoons vanilla
1 cup graham flour
1 1/2 cups all-purpose flour
3 cups uncooked oats
   (quick or old-fashioned)
1 1/2 teaspoons baking soda
1/2 teaspoon salt
1 teaspoon cinnamon
1/2 teaspoon nutmeg
1 cup of raisins, chocolate chips, or dried fruit

Preheat your oven to 350 degrees. Mix together your butter and sugars until creamy. Add egg whites, vanilla, salt, cinnamon, and nutmeg. Stir well. Slowly add the graham flour, all-purpose flour, and baking soda until well blended. Stir in the oats and raisins (or chocolate chips or dried fruit). Drop rounded teaspoons (or tablespoons if you like bigger cookies) of the batter onto ungreased cookie sheets. Have an adult help you put them in the oven and bake for 9–11 minutes. Let the cookies cool off on the tray for a minute before removing them to a rack to cool off completely. These cookies will keep great in an airtight container for about 1 week—if you can get them to last that long!

Adult Help

Activity 24

Dipped Cookie Pops

your favorite cookie recipe
24 lollipop sticks (or Popsicle sticks)
1 bag chocolate chips or butterscotch chips

Make your favorite cookies as you always do, but just before you put them in the oven, poke a stick in one end of each cookie halfway through the dough so that they look just like lollipops. Bake the cookies as directed and allow them to cool completely on waxed paper before going on to the next step. Next, melt your chips in the microwave (see directions for Chocolate Cure-All, page 39). Dip your cookies in the melted chips all the way to the stick. Hold upside down over the bowl for 3 seconds to remove excess chocolate; then return your cookie to the waxed paper to cool off. Repeat until all the cookies are done.

Note: These are great for birthday parties or to give to neighbors at Christmastime.

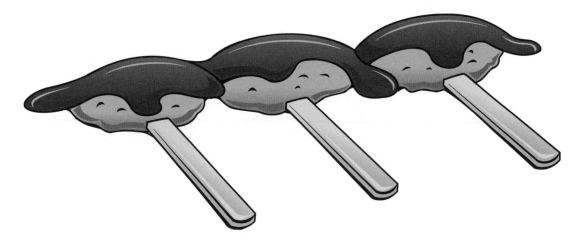

Adult Help

Fun Food Facts

Pat-a-Cake

Pat-a-cake, pat-a-cake, baker's man,
Bake me a cake as fast as you can.
Roll it, and prick it, and mark it with a "B"
And put it in the oven for Baby and me!

This rhyme is used as a fun hand-clapping game (sometimes thought to be a hand-warming exercise) to play with little babies. People today often bake cakes with children's initials marked into them because of this rhyme!

Peter Piper

Peter Piper picked a peck of pickled peppers.
A peck of pickled peppers Peter Piper picked.
If Peter Piper picked a peck of pickled peppers,
How many pickled peppers did Peter Piper pick?

How much is a peck? A peck is the same as 2 gallons, 8 quarts, or 1/4 of a bushel.

Food Far Away—Jerk

When is it okay to call something a "jerk"? When it's jerk chicken (or pork or fish) from Jamaica. Jerk chicken is chicken covered in lime juice, marinated in spices and hot pepper, and barbecued over a pimento-wood fire. Yum!

Food Far Away—Bubble and Squeak

Sometimes foods are named after the way they sound when they are cooking (or after the sounds your stomach makes after eating them!). One food like this is "bubble and squeak," an old dish made in England. It's usually made from potatoes and cabbage fried together, sometimes with beef added, sometimes not. If you ever have the chance to try this dish, listen to it while it's cooking. Do you hear it squeaking as it bubbles merrily away?

FUN FOOD FACTS

Little Jack Horner

Little Jack Horner sat in the corner,
Eating a Christmas pie:
He put in his thumb,
and pulled out a plum,
And said, "What a good boy am I!"

Way back in the 1500s, secret
messages and documents were
sometimes hidden inside of pies to
keep people from stealing them! The
"plum" in this nursery rhyme refers to the deed (papers declaring
ownership) of a really nice piece of property that was taken out of a
pie and kept by Jack Horner in this rhyme.

Peter, Peter, Pumpkin Eater

Peter, Peter, Pumpkin Eater,
Had a wife and couldn't keep her!
He put her in a pumpkin shell,
And there he kept her very well!

Most nursery rhymes have come to America through Europe and
other continents. The "pumpkin" in this nursery rhyme, however, is
from America because pumpkins are native to America. This time,
the Europeans took the words from the Americans!

Marshmallows

Marshmallows are a special treat! Did you know that the ancient
Egyptians ate marshmallows? But not all of the Egyptians—
marshmallows were so special that they were reserved for gods and
royalty. Next time you eat a marshmallow, you can feel like a king or
queen!

FUN FOOD ACTIVITIES

Invent your own recipe! What are some of your favorite foods? Do you think some of them would taste good together? Write a story about what happens when you combine all your favorite foods into one dish. What would it taste like? What would it look like?

_____

_____

_____

_____

_____

_____

_____

_____

_____

_____

_____

_____

_____

_____

FUN FOOD ACTIVITIES

Eating right from morning 'til night! Find your way through the maze. Only cross over foods that are healthy for you until you reach the end of the maze—then it's time for dessert!

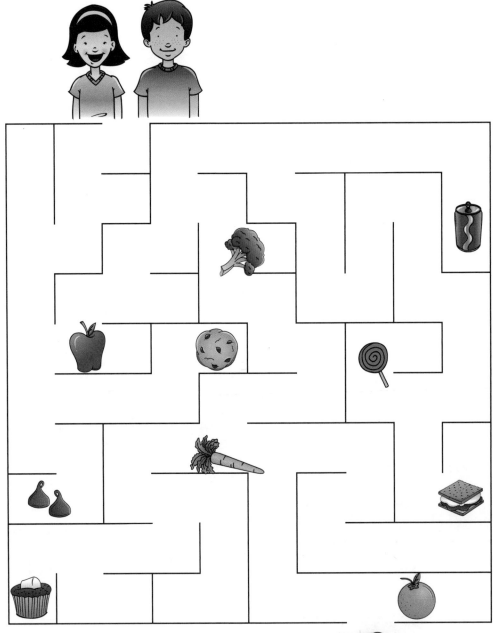

Glossary

Bake—cooking something in an oven

Coat—to roll foods in a mixture or ingredient until all sides are evenly covered with it

Core—to remove the center of something, usually fruits like apples or vegetables like lettuce

Cream—to beat (mix quickly) with a spoon or electric mixer until the ingredients are mixed together and soft and fluffy

Dice—to cut food into little, even pieces, usually pieces that are about 1/4 inch in size

Drain—to remove the water or liquid from a dish, usually by putting the food in a strainer or colander (a bowl with little holes in it)

Drizzle—to slowly pour a liquid ingredient back and forth over food in a small stream

Fold—to combine two ingredients or mixtures into one by turning the mixture over and over from the bottom to the top with each motion

Fry—to cook something in a small amount of oil or fat

Skewer—to put foods on a wooden or metal stick

Spoon—to put an ingredient in a spoon and then over the rest of the food; or, to scoop out the insides of something with a spoon

Sprinkle—to put just a little bit of a topping over something

Stuff—to put a mixture of ingredients inside of something else

Toss—to gently mix ingredients with a lifting motion from the bottom

Whip—to quickly beat ingredients like cream, eggs, or milk to add air into them and make them light and fluffy

Measurements

When cooking, it helps to have a set of measuring cups and spoons. That way, you can put the right amount of ingredients in your recipes, and you'll end up with tasty treats!

cup
8 fluid ounces

dash
the amount that can be picked up between the thumb and two fingers; usually less than 1/8 teaspoon

pinch
the same amount as a dash

spoonful
about one tablespoon

tablespoon
1/2 fluid ounce
2 tablespoons equal 1/8 of a cup

teaspoon
1/6 fluid ounce
3 teaspoons make up one tablespoon